Strong
SIBERIAN HUSKIES

FRIENDLY! ACTIVE! SOCIAL!

PLAYFUL! STRONG! HARDY!

ABDO
Publishing Company

Katherine Hengel

Consulting Editor, Diane Craig, M.A./Reading Specialist

Published by ABDO Publishing Company
8000 West 78th Street, Edina, Minnesota 55439.

Printed in the United States.

Editor: Pam Price
Content Developer: Nancy Tuminelly
Cover and Interior Design and Production:
    Anders Hanson, Mighty Media
Illustrations: Bob Doucet
Photo Credits: Shutterstock

Library of Congress Cataloging-in-Publication Data

Hengel, Katherine.
  Strong Siberian huskies / Katherine Hengel ; illustrated by
Bob Doucet.
    p. cm. -- (Dog daze)
  ISBN 978-1-60453-620-1
  1. Siberian husky--Juvenile literature. I. Title.

  SF429.S65H46 2009
  636.73--dc22
                        2008040974

Super SandCastle™ books are created by a team of
professional educators, reading specialists, and content
developers around five essential components—phonemic
awareness, phonics, vocabulary, text comprehension, and
fluency—to assist young readers as they develop reading
skills and strategies and increase their general
knowledge. All books are written, reviewed, and leveled
for guided reading, early reading intervention, and
Accelerated Reader® programs for use in shared, guided,
and independent reading and writing activities to support
a balanced approach to literacy instruction.

CONTENTS

The
SIBERIAN HUSKY

Siberian huskies are strong, hardworking sled dogs. They can pull light loads for long distances. They are very active and energetic. They can stand cold temperatures because they have very thick coats. These beautiful pack dogs are social and playful, even in the freezing cold!

FACIAL FEATURES

Head

Siberian huskies have round skulls and long **snouts**.

Teeth and Mouth

Siberian huskies have teeth that close in a **scissors bite**.

Eyes

Siberian husky eyes can be blue, brown, or amber. In some huskies, each eye may be a different color.

Ears

Siberian huskies have thick, furry ears that point straight up.

4

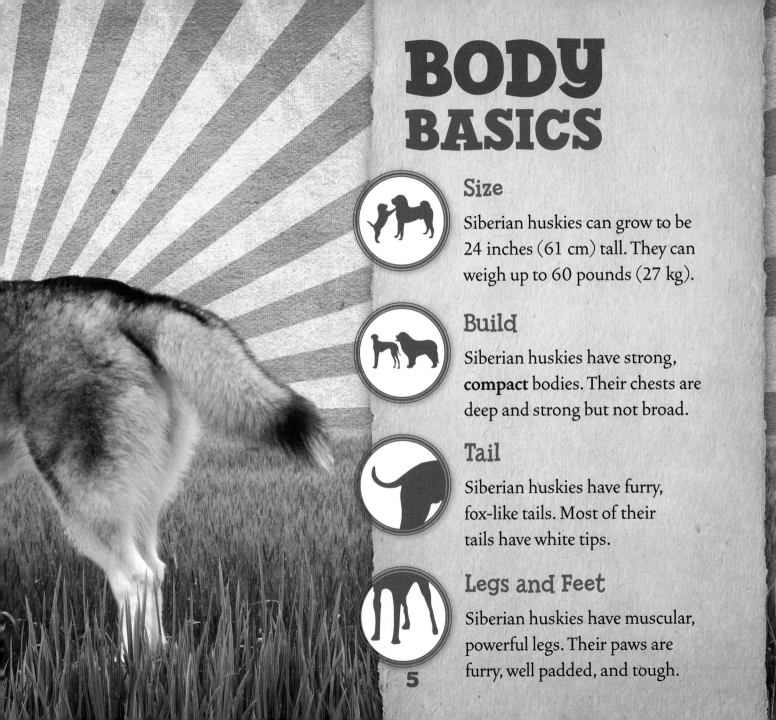

BODY BASICS

Size

Siberian huskies can grow to be 24 inches (61 cm) tall. They can weigh up to 60 pounds (27 kg).

Build

Siberian huskies have strong, **compact** bodies. Their chests are deep and strong but not broad.

Tail

Siberian huskies have furry, fox-like tails. Most of their tails have white tips.

Legs and Feet

Siberian huskies have muscular, powerful legs. Their paws are furry, well padded, and tough.

COAT & COLOR

Siberian Husky Fur

The coat of a Siberian husky has two layers. The undercoat is soft and **dense**. It supports the outer coat, which is smooth and straight. Their thick coats help them handle temperatures as low as −58 degrees Fahrenheit (−50°C). Their bellies are usually white.

WHITE FUR

BLACK FUR

GRAY FUR

RED FUR

Siberian huskies come in many different colors and coats.
The photos on these pages show just a few examples.

WHITE AND BLACK

WHITE AND RED

WHITE AND GRAY

HEALTH & CARE

Life Span

Siberian huskies live about 12 to 15 years.

Grooming

Siberian huskies are easy to groom. Their coats do not need much care. However, twice a year, they will shed a lot and need to be combed thoroughly with a metal comb.

VET'S CHECKLIST

- Siberian huskies should not be left alone outside unless they are inside a yard with a tall fence.

- Make sure your Siberian husky gets plenty of exercise in wide-open spaces.

- Ask your vet which foods are right for your Siberian husky.

- Have your Siberian husky spayed or neutered.

- Visit a vet for regular checkups.

EXERCISE & TRAINING

Activity Level

Siberian huskies have a lot of energy and require a great deal of exercise. They get hyper when they are inactive for a long time. They like to play outside, especially in packs.

Obedience

Siberian huskies are agreeable companions and willing workers. They are very intelligent and trainable, but they also have minds of their own! They can become stubborn and dominant without **consistent** training.

A Few Things You'll Need

A **leash** lets your Siberian husky know that you are the boss. With a leash, you can guide your dog where you want it to go. Most cities require that dogs be on leashes when they are outside.

A **collar** is a strap that goes around your Siberian husky's neck. You can attach a leash to the collar to take your dog on walks. You should also attach an **identification tag** with your home address. If your dog ever gets lost, people will know where it lives.

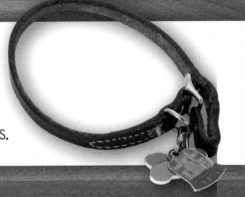

Toys keep your Siberian husky healthy and happy. Dogs like to chase and chew on them.

A **dog bed** will help your pet feel safe and comfortable at night.

ATTITUDE & INTELLIGENCE

Personality

Siberian huskies are friendly, gentle, alert, and outgoing. They are very social animals that don't like to be alone. They aren't very good watchdogs because they love everyone!

Intellect

Siberian huskies are somewhat intelligent. A new command may need to be repeated about 25 to 40 times before the dog learns it.

All About Me

Hi! My name is Sam. I'm a Siberian husky. I just wanted to let you know a few things about me. I made some lists below of things I like and dislike. Check them out!

Things I Like

- Jogging with my owner as long as it is not too hot
- Playing and running with other dogs
- Pulling a sled for long distances with other dogs
- Meeting new people and pets
- Roaming around in open areas

Things I Dislike

- Being ignored all day
- Really hot weather
- Being alone for long periods of time

LITTERS & PUPPIES

Litter Size

Female Siberian huskies usually give birth to four to eight puppies.

Diet

Newborn pups drink their mother's milk. They can begin to eat soft puppy food when they are about five to six weeks old.

Growth

Siberian husky puppies should stay with their mothers until they are eight weeks old. Siberian husky puppies grow until they are about two years old.

BUYING A SIBERIAN HUSKY

Choosing a Breeder

It's best to buy a puppy from a **breeder**, not a pet store. When you visit a dog breeder, ask to see the mother and father of the puppies. Make sure the parents are healthy, friendly, and well behaved.

Picking a Puppy

Choose a puppy that isn't too aggressive or too shy. If you crouch down, some of the puppies may want to play with you. One of them might be the right one for you!

Is It the Right Dog for You?

Buying a dog is a big decision. You'll want to make sure your new pet suits your lifestyle.

Get out a piece of paper. Draw a line down the middle.

Read the statements listed here. Each time you agree with a statement from the left column, make a mark on the left side of your paper. When you agree with a statement from the right column, make a mark on the right side of your paper.

I like to be outside as much as I can.	☑	☐	I don't go outside very often.
I want a dog that likes to spend time with me.	☐	☑	I want a dog that is independent.
I don't want to brush or groom my dog.	☐	☐	I really like brushing and grooming my pets.
I like being active outside in the winter.	☐	☐	I like to live in really warm climates.
A dogsled trip sounds like a lot of fun!	☐	☐	I would never want to travel by sled.
I would like to have more than one dog.	☐	☐	There is no way that I want more than one dog.
I would like to exercise with my dog.	☐	☐	I don't exercise very much.
I don't mind cleaning up dog hair occasionally.	☐	☐	I think shedding is really gross.

If you made more marks on the left side than on the right side, a Siberian husky may be the right dog for you! If you made more marks on the right side of your paper, you might want to consider another breed.

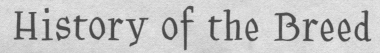

SIBERIA TO ALASKA

Siberian huskies are from Siberia. For centuries, the **Chukchi** people used these dogs to pull sleds and herd reindeer. They were good working dogs that could handle cold, harsh winters.

Siberian huskies were brought to Alaska during the Nome Gold Rush in the early 1900s. Today, Siberian huskies are still very popular as sled dogs. They are also wonderful family pets and show dogs.

Tails of Lore
HUSKY HEROS

In 1903, a Norwegian **musher** named Gunnar Kaasen came to Alaska to look for gold. In 1925, a sickness broke out in Nome, Alaska. To survive, the sick people needed a special medicine. Gunnar and his team of Siberian huskies traveled 600 miles (966 km) through rough ice, dangerous water, and blizzards to bring medicine to Nome.

Gunnar and his dogs saved the city!
This incredible rescue story caught the
attention of the whole nation, and
Siberian huskies became very popular.

FIND THE
SIBERIAN HUSKY

A

B

C

D

THE SIBERIAN HUSKY QUIZ

1. Siberian huskies can stand cold weather. **True or false?**

2. Siberian huskies have furry, fox-like tails. **True or false?**

3. Siberian huskies never have white fur on their bellies. **True or false?**

4. Siberian huskies have a lot of energy. **True or false?**

5. Siberian huskies are not social animals. **True or false?**

6. Siberian Huskies are not from Siberia. **True or false?**

Answers: 1) true 2) true 3) false 4) true 5) false 6) false

GLOSSARY

breed – a group of animals or plants with common ancestors. A *breeder* is someone whose job is to breed certain animals or plants.

Chukchi – a group of people who live in northeast Russia near the Arctic Ocean.

compact – having a body that is short, solid, and not fat.

consistent – being the same each time.

dense – having parts that are crowded together.

musher – one who travels over snow on a sled pulled by dogs.

scissors bite – having lower front teeth that touch the inside of the upper front teeth.

snout – the projecting nose or jaws of an animal's head.

About SUPER SANDCASTLE™

Bigger Books for Emerging Readers
Grades K–4

Created for library, classroom, and at-home use, Super SandCastle™ books support and engage young readers as they develop and build literacy skills and will increase their general knowledge about the world around them. Super SandCastle™ books are part of SandCastle™, the leading preK–3 imprint for emerging and beginning readers. Super SandCastle™ features a larger trim size for more reading fun.

Let Us Know

Super SandCastle™ would like to hear your stories about reading this book. What was your favorite page? Was there something hard that you needed help with? Share the ups and downs of learning to read. We want to hear from you! Send us an e-mail.

sandcastle@abdopublishing.com

Contact us for a complete list of SandCastle™, Super SandCastle™, and other nonfiction and fiction titles from ABDO Publishing Company.

www.abdopublishing.com • 8000 West 78th Street Edina, MN 55439 • 800-800-1312 • 952-831-1632 fax